"PYTHON PLAYBOOK: CODE AND CONQUER - GAMES AND ACTIVITIES EDITION

Contents

4

1. Presentation

1.1 Why Learn Python through Games?

Python is a flexible and fledgling accommodating programming language, settling on it an optimal decision for teenagers to begin their coding process. Learning Python through game advancement makes the interaction charming as well as gives useful, active experience. The following are some compelling arguments for using games as a learning method:

Engagement: Games enamor interest and empower dynamic cooperation, making the growing experience agreeable and vivid.

Creativity: Game advancement permits adolescents to communicate their inventiveness by building their own intuitive universes and characters.

Problem-Solving: Critical thinking skills, which are necessary for programming, are honed in games because they frequently involve complex problem solving.

Moment Satisfaction: Building a game gives unmistakable and prompt outcomes, helping inspiration and certainty.

Application in the Real World: Many programming ideas utilized in game improvement are material to different fields, making learning Python through games a functional decision.

1.2 Who Should Read It
This guide is written specifically for teenagers between the ages of 13 and 18 who are interested in learning programming with a focus on game development. It accepts no earlier coding experience, making it

reasonable for fledglings. The substance is intended to be connecting with and sufficiently moving to catch the interest of youngsters while giving a strong groundwork in Python programming.

1.3 Requirements

Prior to jumping into Python game turn of events, having a couple of requirements in place is fundamental. Although no prior knowledge of programming is required, it is helpful to be familiar with the fundamentals of computer operation. Guarantee the accompanying requirements are met:

Admittance to a PC: Teenagers ought to approach a PC or PC for involved coding works out.

Web Association: A steady web association is essential for downloading Python and related instruments.

Interest and Energy: Energy to investigate and learn is the most important essential. Coding should be approached by teens with an open and curious mind.

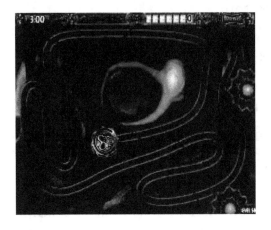

2. Setting up Python Climate
2.1 Introducing Python

Before we begin coding, how about we set up the Python climate on your PC. Follow these moves toward introduce Python:

Windows:

Go to the official Python website.
Download the most recent form of Python.
When you run the installer, check the box that says "Add Python to PATH" to start the installation.
Click "Introduce Now" and adhere to the on-screen guidelines.
Mac:

Macintosh PCs typically accompany Python pre-introduced. Type python3 into the Terminal to see if it has been installed. If not, you can

introduce it utilizing Homemade libation: install Python with brew.
Linux:

Open a terminal and utilize the bundle director well defined for your dispersion (e.g., sudo able get introduce python3 for Ubuntu).
Type python --version or python3 --version into a terminal or command prompt to confirm the installation.

2.2 Choosing a Code Editor

Choosing the right code editor is essential for having a good time coding. The following are a couple of well known choices reasonable for novices:

Code in Visual Studio: a powerful, lightweight editor with excellent Python support. You can get it here.

PyCharm: a Python-specific integrated development environment (IDE) with more features. The People group version is free and can be downloaded here.

IDLE: Python comes with this basic IDE included. It can be used for straightforward projects and is appropriate for novices.

Pick the supervisor that suits your inclinations and introduce it on your PC.

2.3 Prologue to Virtual Conditions

Virtual conditions assist with overseeing conditions and seclude project conditions. Follow these moves toward establish a virtual climate:

Open a terminal or order brief.

Using the cd command, go to the directory of your project.

Run the accompanying order to establish a virtual climate:

Python -m venv venv (You might use Python3 instead of Python on some systems.)

Get the virtual environment going:

Windows:
Copy code and activate scripts on Mac and Linux:
slam
Duplicate code
source venv/receptacle/initiate
You'll see the virtual climate name in your terminal brief whenever it's actuated.

3. Key Python Thoughts
3.1 Variables and Data Types

Factors:

In Python, factors are used to store and administer data. Values are held inside them. An easy example is:

```python
Copy code
name = "John"
age = 16
level = 1.75
```

name is a variable taking care of a string.

age is a whole number putting away factor.

level is a variable taking care of a floating point number.

Information Organizations:

Python works with various information types, for example,

3.2 Control Flow (if statements, loops)

Int (integer), Float (number with floating point), String (string), and Boolean (boolean) are the following types of variables:

In your code, you can go with choices utilizing contingent proclamations.

Python duplicate code: 16 if older than 18:

```
   print("You are an adult.")
else:
   print("You are a minor.")
```

Loops:

Circles help in task redundancy. The two primary types are: circles for and keeping in mind that

Circle for:

python

```
Copy code
for I in range(5):
    while circle: print(i)
```

```python
Copy code
count = 0
while count < 5:
    print(count) count  1
```

3.3 Modules and Capabilities:

Capabilities are code impedes that can be reused. They play out an undertaking, get an outcome, and take in input.

```python
Copy code
def greet(name):
    print("Hello, " + name + "!")

greet("Alice")
Modules:
```

Modules are records with Python code in them. A module can be used to incorporate capabilities and factors into your program.

python
Copy code
# Make a module named mymodule.py
# mymodule.py
def say_hello():
    print("Hello from mymodule!")

Use the module in your chief program

```
import mymodule

mymodule.say_hello()
```

3.4 Records and Word references

Records:

Records are used to store a variety of data in a single variable.

Python Duplicate code for organic products = ["apple," "banana," and "orange"] print(fruits[1] # Getting to the components by recording fruits.append("grape") # Adding a component Word references:

Information is put away in word references as key-esteem matches.

Python duplicate code for an individual = "name": Alice",
   "age": 25,
   "city":   "   Wonderland"
print(person["age"]) # Utilizing a key to get to a worth person["job"]

= "Specialist" # Adding another key-esteem pair Understanding these principal thoughts will give you a strong starting point for making games in Python. In the accompanying fragment, we'll apply these plans to make clear text-based games, ceaselessly growing the complexity of our errands.

4. Making Text-Based Games

4.1 Straightforward Number Speculating Game

We should begin with an essential number speculating game:

```python
Duplicate code
import arbitrary

def number_guessing_game():
    attempts = 0 print("Welcome to the Number Guessing Game!")
secret_number = random.randint(1, 100)
    print("I'm thinking about a number somewhere in the range of 1 and 100.")

    while Valid:
        guess is equal to int(input, "Take a guess:"))
```

```python
        attempts equals one if guess
equals secret_number:
        print(f"Congratulations! You
speculated    the    number    in
{attempts} endeavors.")
        break the elif guess with the
secret number:
        print("Too low! Try once
more.
    else:
        print("Too high! Attempt
once more.")

number_guessing_game()
```

4.2 Executioner

Presently, we should make a straightforward message based Executioner game:

```python
python
Duplicate code
import irregular
```

```python
def choose_word():
    words = ["python", "executioner",
"designer",          "programming",
"game"]
    return random.choice(words)


def executioner():
    attempts = 6  print("Welcome to
Hangman!")    word_to_guess    =
choose_word()  guessed_letters   =
set()
    while True, display_word = ['_'] *
len(word_to_guess).
        print(" ".join(display_word))
        surmise = input("Guess a letter:
")  .lower()  in  the  event  that  you
guess in guessed_letters:
            print("You          previously
speculated that letter. Attempt once
more.")
            proceed

        guessed_letters.add(guess)
```

```python
    on the off chance that
supposition in word_to_guess:
        for i in the following range:
        in the event that
word_to_guess[i] == surmise:
            display_word[i]          =
surmise
    else:
        attempts  -=  one  print(f:
"Incorrect! Attempts remaining:
attempts) if "_" is not present in
display_word:
        print("Congratulations! You
had the word right.")
        break

    if endeavors == 0:
        "Sorry, you ran out of
attempts." print(f The word was
'{word_to_guess}'.")
        break
```

executioner()

4.3 Text-Based Experience Game

Presently, we should make a straightforward message based experience game:

python
Duplicate code

```python
def adventure_game():
    print("Welcome to the Text-Based Experience Game!")
    print("You've arrived in a strange land. Be careful in your choices.")

    while Valid:
        decision = input("Do you need to go left or isn't that so? ") .lower()

        if decision == "left":
            print("A friendly dragon appears to you. It guides you securely.")
```

```
        break   elif   choice   equals
"right":
        print("You coincidentally find
a dim cavern. It prompts an obscure
objective.")
        print("A goliath bug shows
up! You need to battle or escape.")

        activity = input("Do you need
to battle or escape? ") .lower()

        on the off chance that activity
== "battle":
            "You defeat the spider and
continue your journey" is printed.
        break
        elif activity == "escape":
        print ("You find another
way to get away from the spider.")
        break
        else:
        print("Incorrect   selection.
Attempt once more.")
```

```
    else:
        print("Incorrect      selection.
Attempt once more.")
```

adventure game() is a fun way to learn basic Python concepts through text-based games. As adolescents become OK with coding, urge them to improve and redo the games or even make new ones!

5. Introduction to Pygame

5.1 Installing Pygame

The Pygame library must be installed before you can begin developing Pygame. Run: in a terminal or command prompt.

This command will install Pygame and its dependencies. bash Copy code pip install pygame You can begin creating interactive games as soon as it is installed!

5.2 Making a Basic Pygame Window

We should make a fundamental Pygame window:

Python Copy code import pygame import sys # Initialize Pygame pygame.init() # Set the display's width and height to 800 and 600 pixels   screen   =

```
pygame.display.set_mode((width,
height)) # Set the display's caption
to "My Pygame Window" # Run the
main game loop while true:
    for        occasion        in
pygame.event.get():
        if event.type == pygame. QUIT:
            pygame.quit()
            sys.exit()

    # Update the game state here

    # Draw on the screen
    screen.fill((255, 255, 255)) # Fill
the screen with white
    pygame.display.flip()  # Update
the presentation
```

This code instates Pygame, makes a window, and sets up an essential game circle that handles stopping the game when the window is shut.

5.3 Taking care of Occasions (console, mouse)

We should add occasion dealing with for console and mouse input:

```python
Duplicate code
# Inside the game circle
for occasion in pygame.event.get():
    if event.type equals pygame QUIT:
        pygame.quit(), sys.exit(), and
    elif event.type are equivalent to pygame. KEYDOWN:
        on the off chance that event.key == pygame. K_ESCAPE:
            pygame.quit()
            sys.exit()
        elif event.key == pygame. K_SPACE:
            print("Spacebar squeezed!")
    elif event.type == pygame. MOUSEBUTTONDOWN:
```

```python
    if event.button == 1: # Left mouse button
        print("Left mouse button clicked!")
        Event.button == 3 in elif: # Right mouse button
        print("Right mouse button clicked!")
```

This code tunes in for console and mouse occasions inside the game circle. The event handling can be altered in accordance with the requirements of your game.

5.4 Drawing Shapes and Pictures

Presently, how about we draw a few shapes and pictures on the window:

```python
python Copy code # Within the game loop screen.fill((255, 255, 255)) # Draw a rectangle pygame.draw.rect(screen, (0, 0,
```

255), (50, 50, 100, 50)) # (surface, color, rect) # Draw a circle pygame.draw.circle(screen, (255, 0, 0), (200, 200, 30)) # (surface, color, center, radius) # Load and Always substitute the path to your own image file for "image.png."

PRINCESS PYTHON

6. Making Natural Undertakings
6.1 Making a Pong Game

We ought to start by making a direct Pong game using Pygame:

```
python Duplicate code import pygame import sys # Instate Pygame pygame.init() # Set the component's width and level to 800 and 600 pixels screen = pygame.display.set_mode((width, level))
pygame.display.set_caption("Pong Game") # Varieties dull = (0, 0, 0) white = (255, 255, 255) # Oar paddle_width, paddle
 for event in pygame.event.get():
in the event that keys[pygame] paddle_x is under 5, K_RIGHT] and paddle_x < width - paddle_width:
 paddle_x += 5

# Move the ball
```

```
ball_x += ball_speed_x
ball_y += ball_speed_y

# Skirt off the walls
on the off chance that ball_x <= 0 or
ball_x >= width - ball_size:
```

player_y + fall_speed # If player_y > level - player_height, check for crashes with the ground: python Copy code import pygame import sys import erratic # Present Pygame with pygame.init() # Set up the show by utilizing pygame.display.set_mode((width, level)) and pygame.display.set_caption("Space Intruders Clone") # Varieties dim = (0, 0, 0) and white = (255, 255, 255) # player for the occasion in

```
on the off chance that event.type ==
pygame. QUIT:
```

```
sys.exit()    and    pygame.quit()
```
assuming event.type is equivalent to pygame. KEYDOWN:
```
if event.key == pygame. K_SPACE
and bullet_state == "ready":
bullet_x    =    player_x    +
player_width//2 - bullet_width//2
bullet_y = player_y
bullet_state = "release"
```

```
keys = pygame.key.get_pressed()
```
in the event that keys[pygame. player_x and K_LEFT]:
```
if player_x = 5 in keys [pygame]
K_RIGHT], and parcel the player_x
```
width by the player_width to get:
```
player_x    =    5    # Move your
```
opponent. Accepting that enemy_y is higher than level, it approaches enemy_speed.
```
# Move the slug if bullet_state rises
to "discharge": enemy_y is zero, and
```

enemy_x is random.randint(0, enemy_width - width).

Accepting that bullet_y is unaffected, bullet_y is drawing near to bullet_speed:

```
pygame.draw.rect(screen, white,
(player_x, player_y, player_width,
player_height))
pygame.draw.rect(screen, white,
(bullet_x, bullet_y, bullet_width,
bullet_height))
pygame.display.flip() # Update the
element.
```

7. Prologue to Cup

Cup is a Python-based lightweight web application system that can be used with Web Advancement with Jar

7.1. By giving apparatuses, libraries, and examples for building web applications, it simplifies web improvement.
Carafe is momentarily portrayed in the accompanying:

Install Flask in your terminal or command prompt with the following command:

hammer
Copy code
pip present Carafe
Hey World Model:
Make the accompanying substance in the app.py record:

python
Copy code
from carafe import Container

```python
application = Flask(__name__)

@app.route('/')
def hello_world():
    "Hello, World!" return
```

The "Hi, World!" message can be viewed at http://localhost:5000 in your program. message.

7.2 Build a Basic Web Application
We need to create a basic Carafe web application with a variety of courses and formats:

Coordinator Development:
You should make a folder for your project. Make an envelope for HTML layouts inside the organizer.

Organization of Files:

```
project_folder/
app.py
```

designs/
home.html
about.html
app.py:

```python
Copy code
from container import Flask, render_template

application = Flask(__name__)

@app.route('/')
def home():
    return render_template('home.html')

@app.route('/about')
def about():
```

duplicate code in html! DOCTYPE html> html lang="en"> head> meta charset="UTF-8"> meta name="viewport" content="width=device-width, starting scale=1.0"> p>This is the about page./p> /body> /html> Run the Application:

Utilizing python app.py, run the application. To see the different pages, explore to http://localhost:5000 and http://localhost:5000/about in your program.

7.3 Organizing Python with HTML/CSS

Could we redesign our Container application by passing data from Python to HTML and adding some CSS styles:

Modify app.py:

```python
Copy code
```

```python
from cup import Carafe, render_template

application = Flask(__name__)

@app.route('/')
def home():
    title = 'Welcome to the Greeting page!'
    return render_template('home.html', title=title)

@app.route('/about')
def about():
    if 'main' and 'name' are equivalent:
    app.run(debug=True)
```
Change home.html:

html
Copy code

```
<! DOCTYPE html> html lang="en">
head>    meta    name="viewport"
content="width=device-width,
initial-scale=1.0"> title> title/title>
link    rel="stylesheet"    href="
url_for('static',
filename='style.css')">       /head>
body> h1> title/h1> /body>
```

Create a file with your CSS styles called style.css inside the static envelope.

```
css Body of duplicate code; textual
style family: Arial, sans-serif;
   shade of foundation: # f0f0f0;
h1 variety: number 333;
```

Begin the Application:

Utilizing python app.py, run the application. As of now, your Container application integrates a CSS layout and passes data from Python to HTML.

8. Information Perception

8.1 Tasks: Involving Matplotlib to Make Diagrams and Graphs

As a beginning stage, we should check out at the essentials of utilizing Matplotlib. Suppose you need to show information in a visual manner. For instance:

```python
Duplicate code
import matplotlib.pyplot as plt

# Test information
orders = ['Category A', 'Gathering B', 'Class C', 'Request D']
values = [25, 50, 30, 45]

# Reference graph
plt.bar(categories, values, color='skyblue')
plt.xlabel('Categories')
plt.ylabel('Values')
```

```
plt.title('Bar Diagram Model')
plt.show()
```

Investigate different kinds of diagrams like line outlines, pie frames, and spread plots utilizing Matplotlib's flexible capacities.

8.2 Using Folium to Create Intelligent Guides

Folium is a Python library that makes it easier to display information that is controlled by Python on a simple pamphlet map. Utilizing: to set up Folium

hammer
Duplicate code
pip present folium
Here is an unmistakable model:

Python Import Folium by duplicating the code. # Center a map at a specific point with my_map = folium. Using Map(location=[37.7749, -122.4194], zoom_start=12), add a marker to the guide folium. Marker(location=[37.7749, -122.4194], popup='San Francisco').add_to(my_map) # Save the guide to a HTML record my_map.save('map.html') To view the user-friendly guide, open the generated map.html document in a browser.

8.3 Using Pandas to Examine and Control

Data Pandas have particular strengths in this area. You can utilize it to load, clean, and dissect datasets. A simple model is:

Python: Import the code into Pandas as pd # Create a DataFrame

with data = "Name": ['] Alice', 'Weave', 'Charlie', 'David'],
df = pd. DataFrame(data) # Show the DataFrame print(df) # Basic information print(df.describe()) # Plotting the Data df.plot(x='Name', y='Age', kind='bar', color='skyblue', title='Age Course') plt.show() This model uses Matplotlib to create a bar chart, a DataFrame, and basic information.

9. Version Control and Collaborative Coding

9.1 An Overview of Git and GitHub Git:

Git is a system for distributed version control that lets multiple developers work on a project at the same time. It tracks changes, works with joint effort, and oversees various renditions of a codebase.

GitHub:

Git is the version control system used by the web-based platform GitHub. It gives a cooperative climate to engineers to host and survey code, oversee tasks, and fabricate programming together.

Beginning:

Introduce Git: Download and introduce Git from git-scm.com.

Make a GitHub Record: Log in to GitHub.

Set Up Git: Make your email and name settings with:

slam

Duplicate code

git config - - worldwide user.name "Your Name"

git config - - worldwide user.email "your.email@example.com"

9.2 Teaming up on a Straightforward Task

We should make a basic cooperative undertaking on GitHub and team up on it.

Make Another Vault:

Create a new repository on GitHub. Instate it with a README.md record.

Clone the Store:

Clone the vault to your nearby machine utilizing:

Changes can be made using bash, git clone, and https://github.com/your-username/repository-name.git.

Make another branch for your changes:
slam
Duplicate code
git checkout - b include branch
Make changes to the venture documents.
Accept Changes:

Make your changes permanent:
slam
Duplicate code
git add .
Push Changes to GitHub: git commit -m "Add feature X"

Send your modifications to GitHub:

Create a Pull Request: bash copy code git push origin feature-branch

Go to the store on GitHub.
Make a draw demand for your branch.
Audit and Union:

Your changes in the pull request can be reviewed by collaborators.
After endorsement, consolidate the progressions into the principal branch.
Sync Neighborhood Store:

Sync your neighborhood storehouse with the progressions on GitHub:
You have successfully collaborated on a project using Git and GitHub by following these steps: bash Copy

code git pull origin main Version control and collaborative coding are fundamental components of this workflow in software development. Investigate Git's stretching, blending, and compromise highlights for a more profound comprehension.

10. High level Themes for Additional Investigation

10.1 Article Arranged Programming (OOP)

Why OOP:

In order to design and construct applications, Object-Oriented Programming (OOP) is a paradigm that makes use of objects that bundle data and methods that operate on the data. OOP gives a method for organizing code for seclusion, reusability, and versatility.

Key Ideas:

Objects and Classes: The blueprints for objects are set by classes. Objects are cases of classes.

Encapsulation: Packaging information and strategies that

work on the information inside a solitary unit (class).

Inheritance: Reusing code by creating new classes from existing classes.

Polymorphism: utilizing a single interface to represent various object types.

Example:

```python
Duplicate code
class Creature:

    def speak(self):
        pass the class Dog:
    def speak(self):
        return "Woof!"


Cat (Animal) class:
    def speak(self):
        "Meow!" in return
```

```
canine = Dog("Buddy")
feline = Cat("Whiskers")

print(dog.speak()) # Result: Woof!
print(cat.speak()) # Result: Meow!
```

10.2 Using APIs The API, or Application Programming Interface, is as follows:

A Programming interface permits different programming frameworks to speak with one another. The data formats and methods that applications can use to request and exchange information are defined by APIs.

Basic Ideas:

Soothing APIs: Most current APIs follow REST (Illustrative State Move) standards.

HTTP Techniques: Normal techniques incorporate GET

(recover), POST (make), PUT (update), Erase (erase).

Authentication: APIs frequently require OAuth, API keys, or token authentication.

Example:

Utilizing Python to collaborate with a speculative Peaceful Programming interface:

```
Python Copy code import requests
have the following parameters:
"key":"                url       =
"https://api.example.com/data"
your-programming interface key"}

reaction    =    requests.get(url,
params=params)

in    the    event    that
response.status_code == 200:
   information = response.json()
   print(data)
```

```
else:
    print(f"Error:                {
response.status_code}")
```

10.3 Prologue to AI with Python

AI (ML):

AI is a subset of man-made reasoning that spotlights on building frameworks that can gain from information. Python is a well known language for ML because of its broad libraries and structures.

Basic Ideas:

Regulated Learning: Preparing a model utilizing marked information.

Unsupervised Instruction: Tracking down designs in information without marked results.

Public Libraries: scikit-learn for general ML assignments,

TensorFlow and PyTorch for profound learning.

Example:

Creating a straightforward linear regression model with scikit-learn:

```python
Python Copy code from sklearn.model_selection import train_test_split import linear regression import mean squared error import pandas as pd # Sample data data = 'X': [ 1, 2, 3, 4, 5], 'Y': [ 2, 4, 5, 4, 5]}
df = pd. DataFrame(data) # Divide the data into training and testing sets X_train, X_test, y_train, y_test = train_test_split(df[['X']], df['Y'], test_size=0.2, random_state=42) # Create a linear regression model model = LinearRegression() # Train the model model.fit(X_train, y_train) # Make predictions on the test set predictions = mse}')
```

Final talk

Opportunities for investigation and learning Beginning with the essentials of programming in Python, you can progressively progress to additional complicated points, including web improvement, information representation, and AI. Cooperative coding utilizing adaptation control frameworks like Git and GitHub is fundamental for certifiable programming advancement.

Keep these important principles in mind as you begin your journey into programming:

Consistent Learning: The field of writing computer programs is continually advancing. Embrace an outlook of persistent figuring out how to remain refreshed with the most recent innovations and patterns.

Practical Training: Apply your insight through active ventures. Constructing certifiable applications sets your comprehension and upgrades critical thinking abilities.

Collaboration: Cooperative coding is a pivotal expertise. Learn how to collaborate with others, share your code, and help open-source projects. Instruments like Git and GitHub are priceless for cooperative turn of events.

Diversification: Investigate different areas inside programming, for example, web improvement, information science, AI, from there, the sky is the limit. Differentiating your range of abilities opens up additional opportunities and permits you to find regions that line up with your inclinations.

Solving Problems: Writing computer programs is essentially about taking care of issues. Develop areas of strength for a settling mentality, break down complex issues into sensible undertakings, and iteratively make progress toward arrangements.

Recollect that missteps and difficulties are fundamental to the educational experience. Feel free to explore, make blunders, and gain from them. Partake in the innovative approach of building, planning, and tackling issues through code.